Waynesburg College
Waynesburg, Pa. 15370

HALF
PROMISED
LAND

Also by Thomas Lux:

The Land Sighted (chapbook) 1970
Memory's Handgrenade 1972
The Glassblower's Breath 1976
Versions Of Campana (chapbook: translations) 1977
Madrigal on the Way Home (chapbook) 1977
Sunday 1979
Like a Wide Anvil from the Moon the Light (chapbook) 1980
Massachusetts (chapbook) 1981
Tarantulas on the Lifebuoy (chapbook) 1983

HALF
PROMISED
LAND

THOMAS LUX

HOUGHTON MIFFLIN COMPANY BOSTON 1986

Copyright © 1986 by Thomas Lux
All rights reserved. No part of this work may be reproduced or transmitted in any form or by any means, electronic or mechanical, including photocopying and recording, or by any information storage or retrieval system, except as may be expressly permitted by the 1976 Copyright Act or in writing from the publisher. Requests for permission should be addressed in writing to Houghton Mifflin Company, 2 Park Street, Boston, Massachusetts 02108.

Library of Congress Cataloging-in-Publication Data
Lux, Thomas, date.
  Half promised land.
  I. Title.
PS3562.U87H34 1986   811'.54   85-30506
ISBN 0-395-38255-6
ISBN 0-395-38256-4 (pbk.)

Printed in the United States of America
Q 10 9 8 7 6 5 4 3 2 1

"The Life" by James Wright, copyright © 1968 by James Wright. Reprinted from *Shall We Gather at the River* by permission of Wesleyan University Press.

The poems in this volume first appeared in the following magazines: *American Poetry Review*: "The Great Books of the Dead." *Atlantic Monthly*: "Snake Lake." *Crazy Horse*: "Night Above the Town," "Pedestrian." *Field*: "His Job Is Honest and Simple," "Like a Wide Anvil from the Moon the Light," "The Dark Comes On in Blocks, in Cubes," "There Were Some Summers," "Triptych, Middle Panel Burning." *Ironwood*: "Sailing, Islands." *Memphis State Review*: "Empty Pitchforks." *Paris Review*: "Sleepmask Dithyrambic," "Somebody's Aunt Swabbing Her Birdbath," "The Thirst of Turtles." *Pequod*: "Early On, This Decade's Light Smelled," "If I Die Before I Wake," "It Must Be the Monk in Me." *Ploughshares*: "Hospital View," "On Resumption of the Military Draft," "Tarantulas on the Lifebuoy," "The Milkman and His Son." *Poetry*: "After a Few Whiffs of Another World," "His Spine Curved Just Enough." "It's the Little Towns I Like," "The Night So Bright a Squirrel Reads." *Rubicon*: "Dr. Goebbels's Novels," "When I'm Gone." *Seneca Review*: "A Tenth of a Cent a Stitch," "The Crows of Boston and New York," "The Fourth Grade," "The Swimming Pool," "*Via Posthumia*," "Wife Hits Moose." *Sonora Review*: "At the Far End of a Long Wharf," "Beneath the Apple Branches Bent Dumbly," "Moon-Annoyed, Cognac's Ashen Thrill," "The Oxymoron Sisters," "You Go to School to Learn."

   Many of these poems also appeared in the following chapbooks: *Like a Wide Anvil from the Moon the Light* (Black Market Books); *Massachusetts* (Pym-Randall Books); *Tarantulas on the Lifebuoy* (&Ampersand).

The author would like to thank the National Endowment for the Arts, the Mellon Foundation, the Poetry Society of America (for the Alice Fay Di Castagnola Award), and the MacDowell Colony.

Special thanks to Michael Ryan, Jorie Graham, and Laura Nash.

— for Jean

CONTENTS

I

The Milkman and His Son · 3
Empty Pitchforks · 5
Night Above the Town · 6
Sailing, Islands · 7
The Crows of Boston and New York · 8
The Fourth Grade · 10
Sleepmask Dithyrambic · 12
The Thirst of Turtles · 14
Sleep for Bears · 16
Somebody's Aunt Swabbing Her Birdbath · 17
Give It to the Wind · 18
Tarantulas on the Lifebuoy · 19

II

Early On, This Decade's Light Smelled · 23
His Job Is Honest and Simple · 24
It's the Little Towns I Like · 25
At the Far End of a Long Wharf · 26
The Night So Bright a Squirrel Reads · 27
You Go to School to Learn · 28
If I Die Before I Wake · 29
There Were Some Summers · 30
His Spine Curved Just Enough · 31
Moon-Annoyed, Cognac's Ashen Thrill · 32
It Must Be the Monk in Me · 33
After a Few Whiffs of Another World · 34

The Dark Comes On in Blocks, in Cubes · 35
Like a Wide Anvil from the Moon the Light · 36
Beneath the Apple Branches Bent Dumbly · 37

III

Hospital View · 41
The Oxymoron Sisters · 42
Dr. Goebbels's Novels · 44
A Tenth of a Cent a Stitch · 46
The Great Books of the Dead · 47
On Resumption of the Military Draft · 48
When I'm Gone · 49
The Swimming Pool · 50
Via Posthumia · 52
Snake Lake · 53
Wife Hits Moose · 54
Pedestrian · 55

IV

Triptych, Middle Panel Burning · 59

It is the old loneliness.
It is.
And it is.
The last time.

— *James Wright*

I

THE MILKMAN AND HIS SON
(for my father)

For a year he'd collect
the milk bottles — those cracked,
chipped, or with the label's blue
scene of a farm

fading. In winter
they'd load the boxes on a sled
and drag them to the dump

which was lovely then: a white sheet
drawn up, like a joke, over
the face of a sleeper.
As they lob the bottles in

the son begs a trick
and the milkman obliges: tossing
one bottle in a high arc,
he shatters it in midair

with another. One thousand astonished
splints of glass
falling . . . Again
and again, and damned
if that milkman,
that easy slinger
on the dump's edge (as the drifted
junk tips its hats

of snow), damned if he didn't
hit almost half! Not bad.
Along with gentleness,

and the sane bewilderment
of understanding nothing cruel,
it was a thing he did best.

EMPTY PITCHFORKS
"There was poverty before money."

There was debtors' prison before inmates,
there was hunger prefossil,

there was pain before a nervous system
to convey it to the brain, there existed

poverty before intelligence, or accountants,
before narration; there was bankruptcy aswirl

in nowhere, it was palpable
where nothing was palpable, there was repossession

in the gasses forming so many billion . . . ;
there was poverty — it had a tongue — in cooling

ash, in marl, and coming loam,
thirst in the few strands of hay slipping

between a pitchfork's wide tines,
in the reptile and the first birds,

poverty aloof and no mystery like God
its maker; there was surely want

in one steamed and sagging onion,
there was poverty in the shard of bread

sopped in the final drop of gravy
you snatched from your brother's mouth.

NIGHT ABOVE THE TOWN

In the glassed-in jazz club acres above
flat streets spoking distant ovals
I think of: Foster Grandparents. Because,
so many stories below, isolated,
oxygen-starved on asphalt, is a blue
and white Foster Grandparents bus. The tunes
up here are dumb and loud
so I look down
to what I can see: I think
it would be good
to have a foster grandparent, I'll apply
and plead a need for wisdom
and brownies. — Grandma, pinched one,
I want your tin-tasting sharp calm,
come back both grouchy and smart;
Grandfather, distanced,
disinherit me, pass again your cool palms
along the flats of my head . . . I'll apply
tomorrow — if there's a bus
then there's an office
and *slam!* what I'm back to is bad
music, the xylophonist seems to be beating
mice to death, there's a foul
pelican sax and the smell
of youth's pleasant sex and sweat and all
their hundreds of feet on the floor
and fists keeping time
on the tables . . . Grandmother. Grandfather.

SAILING, ISLANDS
(for Geoffrey Wolff)

Off the coast the islands anchor — small,
wavery, green-blond in early spring,
like the heads, from here, because of their fineness,
their fragility, of babies. Why *this*
comparison? Continents, large landmasses
as metaphor equal adults and islands

broken off, parts of a whole, equal babies?
Oh, I don't think so. Maybe it's more
that sailing — ancient, creaky — on seawater
fixes in me some blistering joy,
some fear I want to eat,
embrace — like a baby broken off

from my own body. The islands huddle,
but do not drown, at the entrance
of the bay. *Imagination
is a terrible thing: you will need
to love it,* I will teach
my son or daughter.

THE CROWS OF BOSTON AND NEW YORK

You've seen them, these semiurban birds
who live, not in, but on the edge of great cities.
No longer wild — of the cornfield, or resting high
in rafters of deserted tobacco barns. They venture
to the borders, but will not cross, where city sends
its last tendrils out and park gives edge
to woods, where the first lawns
larger than billiard tables grow
each block a little larger
with the houses. These crows

like old and gnarly pines
to graze beneath, aloof, and to sit in. They are not
so bold as smart and seem to know that laws exist
against the discharge of shotguns upon them.
Old blue-black aristocrats, they prefer
to saunter, at midday, across lawns
of pine nuts abundant, the best spots
to steal what lesser birds hold dear.
Maybe this is why a group of them is murder.
They are everywhere where they never used to be.

I hate to see it: a bird so crafty, so sure,
moving in where it's easier to eat
and they grow dim. What logic
sends them here and not so far away
only fieldhands know them? Maybe
they come to us, to live among us

so they can claim it as *their* choice —
which makes them proud and bright,
though does not cease their doom,
nor preserve their haughty, haunting cry.

THE FOURTH GRADE

I suppose that we were shocked
but doubt the reading level dropped
among the members of the Blue Jays
(those between the Eagles and the Crows)
when one of us shot his mother and didn't show
up at school. It's safe to say he wasn't missed.
We didn't like him (he held *my* head
between a door and the jamb and pressed)
but this was something else: shot her dead.

Bobby the lonely
Bobby the mad
shot the only mother he ever had
Shot her and shot her
until she was dead
Like a screen door slamming
the neighbors said

Maybe this is how the habit of metaphor begins.
Maybe it starts with terror up to our chins.
He went away to "a home" until he was old
enough to go to court, and thence to jail.
It would surprise me if he got any mail.
No father was around so the house was sold;
I remember the sign — everybody pointed it out.
It was November, the police done, and it was cold.
Nobody forgave him, especially the brutes and the louts.

Bobby the lonely
Bobby the sad

shot the only mother he ever had
Shot her and shot her
until she was dead
Like a screen door slamming and slamming
the neighbors said

SLEEPMASK DITHYRAMBIC

You must remove your sleepmask, haul it
from your eyes, sleep a white sleep without
slapping floodwaters — let it go,
let its thumbscrews loosen, let it unwind
like bandages (lily-flavored flesh
beneath, pearl-colored the pale
caused by) — lower it: sightseer
in oblivion, all the dumb
joy of death's leaning over happy
tombstones — send it downstream
on sweet pontoons, give it back
to the blanks, fold it like two soft cleavers —
what once ripped your pillow like shrapnel
flesh — what was sleeping
with coal on your eyelids, what's worn
threadbare by black wheels in your forehead,
what deepest blue abided by — let it go —
what screeches like ice pick to ice,
black and padded: Sleepmask the Teacher,
Sleepmask the Round Sky, Sleepmask
Fracture bearing its elastic
into the back of your head, sleepmask black
as pines doused in starlessness — get rid
of it — yours, your spider's
and his spare, your wife's mink one,
your dog's, the miniatures strung like popcorn,
all of them black like the cinders
of flags, blanker than lies, the low
shiver of dog-spume lies, sleepmask that sends
your eyes twirling like apples

in a whipsaw wind: sleepmask glued,
stapled, painted on, pinned,
licked clean, and monogrammed,
sleepmask surgically implanted, sleepmask

congenital, swaddling clothes and bib —
refuse it, remove it — sleepmask an island
overrun with rats and cheese: the formal,
feral, dipped in doom — drop it, tear
it off, lower it like the lid of a coffin
filled with enemy: sleepmask.

THE THIRST OF TURTLES

How parched, how marrow-dust dry
they must get on their long surface and undersea
journeys — huge stuffed husks,
imperturbable swimmers grazing
jellyfish abutting the bruised
waters' pasture. How thirsty
a sixty-day swim, how graceful
the winching back to one unforgotten
shore. *Plub, plub,* sleepless
the hull's inner workings, their tails
motorless rudderings; deep,
deep their thirst and need. One hundred,
one hundred and twenty: how long they live
in their thirst, propelling
the great bloody steaks of their bodies,
dreaming, anticipating alert,
single-purposed oblivions: sweet
sweet turtle-sex — which excites
the lonely watches of sailors — sometimes days
joined in wave-riding rapture on the surface
of the depths. And still more thirsty
afterward, how alone later (currents
having taken) — righted, relentless,
back on course, collision, with centuries,
with a shore: solitary, speechless,
utterly buoyant, as unethereal
as cabbage. How thirsty these
both wise and clumsy, like us, feeding
in ever-widening or diminishing circles,
outward and inward, dropping

great oily tears, killing themselves
to beat a big hole in dirt,
burying something, then retreating
heavily on their own tracks, like rails,
reaching forward to the sea.

SLEEP FOR BEARS
(to Emily Graham Galvin)

Once, you tottered, head-level
with armrest, and my hand
on its swivel known as elbow
dropped down, glad,

and palmed your lighted,
round head. It was soft
and hot. You had no cough
or fever, so it must have been

what goes on in there: bears,
and bananas, and Mom, and Pop,
and bears. I happen to know your mom
has a bag of them (I won't tell where

they're hidden) — multiple,
innumerable bears,
more than you could love, ever.
But — bear by bear, as they appear,

emerge from their bag, I hope you try,
little handwarmer, little globe
of heat and heart, I hope you try
to love and love each lucky one.

SOMEBODY'S AUNT SWABBING
HER BIRDBATH

Somebody's aunt out swabbing her birdbath
with Lysol and the town papermill down the block
is beginning to blister in a clean shock
of light. You drive away. The math

is grammarschool: x thousand workers,
y hundred jobs. The shoe factory closed last year.
Nobody's starving, but the church is in fear
it'll lose some customers.

A man steps out into his backyard's yellow air —
apart from his mortgage, his gripes.
He is perfectly lighted by secret animal stripes.
As you drive away a blunt wind parts his hair.

GIVE IT TO THE WIND

If the wind touches your cheek
in a manner that pleases you,
then to it give something back.
Give some dollars, a good slice
of bread, a phrase from a woman
who loves you; open an ampule
of joy and wave it, out loud.
If you find a dime, then give two
to a beggar, celebrate

nerve endings, your soup.
If whole minutes exist
when to your left is a river with ducks
and to your right a cathedral slashed
by light, then carry clean bandages
to a battlefront, swab foreheads
in a contagious ward; if a few
cells bloom, a synapse heals,
then stab a thousand tiny flags

into the graves of generals,
then mourn a murderer's childhood.
And if, after furious sleep,
the room is windy
and cool air slides across the blank
dunes of your sheet, then thank
the night for the day
and the day for what
it is: liable to be.

18

TARANTULAS ON THE LIFEBUOY

For some semitropical reason
when the rains fall
relentlessly they fall

into swimming pools, these otherwise
bright and scary
arachnids. They can swim
a little, but not for long

and they can't climb the ladder out.
They usually drown — but
if you want their favor,
if you believe there is justice,
a reward for not loving

the death of ugly
and even dangerous (the eel, hog snake,
rats) creatures, if

you believe these things, then
you would leave a lifebuoy
or two in your swimming pool at night.

And in the morning
you would haul ashore
the huddled, hairy survivors

and escort them
back to the bush, and know,
be assured that at least these saved,
as individuals, would not turn up

again someday
in your hat, drawer,
or the tangled underworld

of your socks, and that even —
when your belief in justice
merges with your belief in dreams —
they may tell the others

in a sign language
four times as subtle
and complicated as man's

that you are good,
that you love them,
that you would save them again.

II

EARLY ON, THIS DECADE'S LIGHT SMELLED

Early on, this decade's light smelled
like something burning and now
of something smoldering, the end
of the decade smells: the grave, forever
lingering of limb-smell exploded, some
bodies, many, of our generation blown
every which way, gone. And choking
on that smell we created another: the faint,
exhausted, perfumed puffs of ennui. A whole
generation looking over its shoulder
retromancing nothing, using the peripheral
(nothing), and forward? The future.
It's arrived — forgetfulness, jobs,
even some money, which we didn't want,
but which we got, our actual share,
actually. To purchase amnesia
it doesn't take much. — We could count
the dead and they would be mostly
men, and then we could count the women,
mostly alive, whose turn it is now,
nailing down each day with an X
of something done on a calendar
creeping toward a new century.

1979

HIS JOB IS HONEST AND SIMPLE

His job is honest and simple: keeping
the forest tidy. He replaces,
after repairing, the nests
on their branches, he points every pine needle north,
polishes the owl's stained perch,
feather-dusts the entrance
to the weasel's burrow, soft-brushes
each chipmunk (the chinchilla
of the forest banal), buffs antlers, gives
sympathy to ragweed, tries to convince —
like a paternal and inept psychiatrist —
the lowly garter snake to think
of himself, as he parts the grass,
as an actor parting the stage curtain
to wild applause, arranges, in the clearing,
the great beams of light . . . This is his job: a day's,
a week's, a life's calm, continuous,
low-paying devotion. At dawn
he makes a few sandwiches and goes
to work. *I love this,* he thinks as he passes
the wild watercress — its green as stunning
as surviving a plane crash — in the small,
inaccessible swamp.

IT'S THE LITTLE TOWNS I LIKE

It's the little towns I like,
with their little mills making ratchets
and stanchions, elastic web,
spindles, you
name it. I like them in New England,
America, particularly — providing
bad jobs good enough to live on, to live in
families even: kindergarten,
church suppers, beach umbrellas . . . The towns
are real, so fragile in their loneliness
a flood could come along
(and floods have) and cut them in two,
in half. There is no mayor,
the town council's not prepared
for this, three of the four policemen
are stranded on their roofs . . . and it doesn't stop
raining. The mountain
is so thick with water, parts of it just slide
down on the heifers — soggy, suicidal —
in the pastures below. It rains, it rains
in these towns and, because
there's no other way, your father gets in a rowboat
so he can go to work.

At the far end of a long wharf
a deaf child, while fishing, hauls in
a large eel and — not
because it is ugly — she bashes its brains
out of eeldom on the hot
planks — *whamp, whamp, whamp,* a sound
she does not hear. It's the distance
and the heat that abstracts
the image for me. She also does not hear,
nor do I, the splash the eel makes
when she tosses it in her bucket,
nor do we hear the new bait
pierced by the clean hook, nor
its lowering into the water again.
Nobody could. I watch her
all afternoon until, catching nothing
else, she walks the wharf toward
me, her cousin, thinking
with a thousand fingers. Pointing
at our boat she tells me
to drag it to the water. She wants me to row
her out to the deep lanes of fish.
Poetry is a menial task.

THE NIGHT SO BRIGHT A SQUIRREL READS

The night so bright a squirrel reads
a novel on his branch
without clicking on his lamp.
You know you're in a forest — the stars,
the moon blaring
off the white birch . . . You could walk
out with your wife
into the forest, toward the fields beyond,
you could walk apart from her,
and still see her. It's so bright
you need not talk nor fear
that particular sticky abrasion you get
by walking into pine trees. You find
a lucidity in this darkness.
Your wife is here — three or four
trees away — you recognize her profile,
and you do not think she is anyone else,
here with you, a hundred
or so yards now from a field where,
in an hour or so, you might see
dawn's first deer browsing, or an owl,
soaring home after the shift he loves,
a fat sack of field mice under his wing.

YOU GO TO SCHOOL TO LEARN

You go to school to learn
to read and add, to someday
make some money. It — money — makes
sense: you need
a better tractor, an addition
to the gameroom, you prefer
to buy your beancurd by the barrel.
There's no other way to get the goods
you need. Besides, it keeps people busy
working — for it.
It's sensible and, therefore, you go
to school to learn (and the teacher,
having learned, gets paid to teach you) how
to get it. Fine. But:
you're taught away from poetry
or, say, dancing ("That's nice, dear,
but there's no dough in it"). No poem
ever bought a hamburger, or not too many. It's true,
and so, every morning — it's still dark! —
you see them, the children, like angels
being marched off to execution,
or banks. Their bodies luminous
in headlights. Going to school.

IF I DIE BEFORE I WAKE

If I die before I wake
I pray the Lord my soul to take . . .
From a common enough
and nondenominational child's prayer.
Not too unlike a lullaby, it's a simple
pledge in verse before hitting
the dark night after night
and one line ringing
a few times in the mind: *If I die*
before I wake. Oh, the generations
of insomniacs created,
the night-light industry booming!
But let's face it: prayer is good,
particularly for children.
They should understand some things
so they might appreciate
them. Like: the buzzards and the bees,
what those stone visors mean,
poking up, on lawns behind fences,
in rows, whitish dominoes . . .
They should know: it's a sleepy journey
to a half promised land
and you never wake at all.

THERE WERE SOME SUMMERS

There were some summers
like this: The blue barn steaming,
some cowbirds dozing with their heads
on each other's shoulders, the electric fences
humming low in the mid-August heat . . .
So calm the slow sweat existing
in half-fictive memory: a boy
wandering from house, to hayloft, to coop,
past a dump where a saddle rots
on a sawhorse, through the still forest
of a cornfield, to a pasture talking to himself
or the bored, baleful Holsteins nodding
beneath the round shade of catalpa, the boy
walking his trail toward the brook
in a deep but mediocre gully,
through skunk cabbage and popweed,
down sandbanks (a descending
quarter-acre Sahara), the boy wandering,
thinking nothing, thinking: *Sweatbox,
sweatbox,* the boy on his way
toward a minnow whose slight beard
tells the subtleties of the current, holding there,
in water cold enough to break your ankles.

HIS SPINE CURVED JUST ENOUGH

His spine curved just enough
to suggest a youth spent amidst a boring
landscape: brokedown corncrib, abandoned sty,
skeletal manure shed, a two-silo barn with one
sold off leaving a round pit
filled with rubble — where once the sweet silage
piled up and up now the brooding
ground of toads. And then the barn
began to buckle like an ancient mule falling
first to one knee, then both,
rear haunches still bravely, barely aloft.
Whatever hay left huddling in corners
more fossil than vegetable.
This landscape exists — in many
places — and is almost lovely,
even in, even in spite of, its decay.
It endures in histories
and in fiction: the crabapple, the gray
pastures, the dried dung
how many years old? — And atop the barn
a weather vane knocked askew by a rifle shot,
pointing straight up, as if all the winds
were going to heaven.

MOON-ANNOYED, COGNAC'S ASHEN THRILL

Moon-annoyed, cognac's ashen thrill
diminishing, irritated by sunlight,
decent sleep, good food, and piles
of money — nothing helps
the heebie-jeebies when they start, like hunger
revving up, when they begin their tossing cruise
beneath the skin, hauling the spine
erect with fear. Nothing. Nothing
helps. What are the origins (embryo,
embryo, where are you going, what
do you know)? Nobody can say,
or will, but it's got to do,
you can bet, with death, which,
some people will tell you, is a part
of life. Right. Personally,
I don't care. It's over you others
I worry, why you worry. How can you fear
what hardly equals the blank wash
of rain on slate shingles,
how can you fear what is not sleep,
what is not quiet, what is sexless,
what has no memory, what lacks
imagination, what does not . . . ?

IT MUST BE THE MONK IN ME

It must be the monk in me,
or the teen-age girl. That's why I'm always off
somewhere in my mind with something
stupid (like a monk) or spiritual
(like a teen-age girl). Sometimes, there's vision,
by reason of faith, in glimpses, or else,
and more often, a lovely blank, a hunger
like Moses' hunger when with his fingernails
he scraped the boulders of their meager lichen
and then fiercely sucking them . . . It's a way
of living on the earth — to be away
from it part of the time. They say
it begins in childhood: your dog
gets runned over, your father
puts a knife to your mother's throat . . .
But those things only make you crazy
and don't account for scanning,
or actually mapping, a galaxy inside. I believe
it happens *before* birth, and has to do,
naturally, with Mom. Not with what she eats,
or does, or even thinks — but with what she *doesn't*
think, or want to: the knot of you growing larger
and, therefore, growing away.

AFTER A FEW WHIFFS OF
ANOTHER WORLD

After a few whiffs of another world
he decided to stay with the stench
of the present: dumpster lids everywhere
rising like cakes, garbage scows
moving in long orderly lines
across the harbor . . . The olfactory — he loves it
even when it wafts, wracking all points
of the compass. It's always invisible
and takes its direction according to the whimsy
of wind, or fans, or the waves
of a hand. Cave dwellers knew it,
and dogs. The bare smell
of dirt on cabbage, the snow-
on-your-arm smell. Even
in the abstract: fear-smell, like spit
on a knife blade. And
what the worms inhale, and then
the smell of dew on barbed wire, the sweet,
thick smell of sex, slick,
our lungs giddy and pink with it . . .
It's not the world which is good or bad
and so we run our noses over everything.
Even the dumb have this sense.

THE DARK COMES ON IN BLOCKS,
IN CUBES

The dark comes on in blocks, in cubes,
in cubics of black measured
perfectly, perfectly
filled. It's subtle and it's not,
depending on your point of view.
You can measure it best in a forest,
or in a grassy lowland, or in any place
where your lamp is the only lamp and you can turn it off.
To describe it the usual adjectives
of the gray/black genre will not do. It's not light,
nor is it the absence of light, but
oh, it's sweet, sweet like ink
dropped in sugar, necessary and invisible
like drafts of oxygen. Absolutely,
in squares, in its containers of space,
the darkness arrives — as daily
as bread, as sad as a haymow
going over and over a stubble field,
as routine as guards
climbing to gun towers
along penitentiary walls, clicking
on their searchlights
against it.

LIKE A WIDE ANVIL FROM THE MOON THE LIGHT

Like a wide anvil from the moon the light
on the cold radiator and all the windows in a row
along the spine close — zeros winding tight.
And to make the rattlesnakes feel at home?
A private cactus farm. There's not an eek's chance
of getting out of here. Some apples, bruised,
mute, are nailed back to their branches,
and the south wind — low, hot ash — cruises
through a crook in the apple tree's trunk.
The dirt, not known for its tenderness, on its knees
somewhat, and one munificent ant carries a crumb
to the crumbless. Every pond on earth agrees:
they are tired of being dragged — all those hooks —
for drowned children. All this beneath
the ceaseless lineage of comets! Books
help a little: groan-soaked, one broken etc. thief,
tree surgeons lost above tree lines,
chasmed sidewalks, a hatful of blanks,
sore-got ore . . . Yes! — it does, it does feel exactly fine
crawling ashore, emptying the boots of water, and frankly
here's to the clouds the color of bone,
here's to the indecipherable path home,
here's to the worm's sweat in the loam . . .

BENEATH THE APPLE BRANCHES BENT DUMBLY

Beneath the apple branches bent dumbly
with the blank weight of their blossoms —
the grass and me — completely
alive with one thought
like a shin struck with an axe: What
is the same each summer? I know
that the ring of cold slung
through my chest grows colder, that the mountains'
lowly crags grow imperceptibly rounder, but what
is the same? Not the driveway
littered (in a few months) with crushed
apples swarmed by yellowjackets — those cruel
insects, not the hackneyed
rock garden, its pool for goldfish
long filled in with dirt and a few
ill-bred petunias, not the heat bugs
and their high whine . . . What
is the *same?* Only the incomparable chins
of horses, only a desire
to place the mural of a pond
horizontal as it belongs,
only the long haul in the linear world,
ongoing.

III

Waynesburg College Library
Waynesburg, Pa.   15370

HOSPITAL VIEW

Across an alley, opposite exactly
my window: Intensive Care Unit. At night I sit
in my dark and stare into its greenly lit
lucidity: I can almost read the x-rays hung
on the wall — two bad ghost pears, the lungs . . .
Plasma bottles glister, beep-machines, a blur
of women and men in white frocks.
On starless nights I can read the clock.
I look because it's there. If,
out my window, I could see flax fields
parted like the haircuts of children,
if outside there were wide arenas of air,
if I could look out and up to a long sky
and study a jet's fading headlines . . . But,
Intensive Care is my view.
I never see them wheel anyone in or out.
They're just there, hooked up, in doubt,
trying to come back. — Come back, clear, still shapes;
hang on however, anonymous flesh,
even though you labor with it. I press
my own body back on my own bed, a wish
on my lips that your lives be again and again
limned by dawn.

THE OXYMORON SISTERS

The Oxymoron sisters, Snowflake and Acetylene,
returned from Camp Hatchet today, pale
and furious, loaded down with camp-
crafted ashtrays and pillowslips,
the sweetlings. You should love them
both: the shy Snowflake,
with her albums and albums
of pressed fern (at age seven,
the family story goes, she petitioned
to change her name to Fern), her neck
like cream, holding in its curve the hope
of a second world, a world aswarm
with passivity, one lacy,
yawn-laden afternoon after another,
wind chimes sonorously lighted . . . *serene*
Snow distant Flake. And then
our Acetylene: taller, nervous, her tack-
hammer fists tattering the air as she talks.
Acetylene the acute, the keen,
in her memory some long blades
hardened by fire. Acetylene — arrested
for arson in kindergarten, pet prank
of filling ice trays with lighter fluid.
They're home from camp today, again
among us and around us, our darlings,
our fearsome sisters inside
and out; these precious, necessary,
these two — both of whom,

despite nominal redemptions,
no matter how much we love them,
both of whom are ugly
and dying.

DR. GOEBBELS'S NOVELS

Dr. Goebbels did not go to heaven. The mundane,
and worse — murderous — literature
of his soul will not come down to us;
not even among the lesser ranks
will this dramatist come down to us
as sometimes the most obscure can do, giving
some sense of what it is,
this walk around on earth. Dr. Goebbels's
novels, plays, and poems
will not be read — not even for insights,
historical, into his character.
His theories about language
were simple: *its best use is for lies.*
This was no monster,
nor was the thing he believed in,
which was nothing. Dr. Goebbels
did not go to heaven, as he wished,
with his wife and six poisoned
babies (4½ to 14!). This was no monster,
being too vain, having no ideas,
and hating the sight of blood.
He showed the world one limit of language
(written or spoken — but always
written first): it can give us
what we need to keep on hating.
Dr. Goebbels did not go to heaven,
nor did he burn in hell.
It was in the chancellery

garden where he burned — an ordinary man,
in ordinary petrol — in fire so hot
that on his bad foot
it warped the brace.

A TENTH OF A CENT A STITCH

Because she did not understand
why mansions make me sad,
because on our coldest streets
tonight, in cardboard boxes, sleep
a thousand men and women, because
for underwear against a rip-tooth wind

they will stuff their rags
with fashion magazines . . . You've heard all this
before: on bluest caviar some people sup,
on liver of goose shimmering, by protein sunk,
in golden aspic, on legs of crab cracked
by wetbacks' hands, etc., while so many

others — what *is* the percentage,
rich to poor? — eat a loaf of bread punched through
with holes. This is all around
and in the history books — which pages
you cannot eat. Never was I a Communist — Marx
and Engels own a string of shoestores

for all I know, and probably do, that gouge
the poor both here and in some land
where the shoes by hand
are sewn: one-tenth of a cent a stitch.
History never has been fair; for only a few
there is no pledge but misery and rue:

breadlines, strikebreakers, slaveships.
Baby starves and father gets the whip.

THE GREAT BOOKS OF THE DEAD

The great books of the dead are, by nature,
upbeat, their interest in an afterlife
in which a place depends on your stature,
how you lived, gave or took, and did you love your wife? —

during *this* life, the one where you read the books.
These familiar volumes, popular at times
when we felt mystical. Mostly we were crooks:
of experience, or on drugs. I drew the line:

the Egyptians didn't give a fuck about me.
From then on it was honest, nothing but what's there:
the sky a blue turtle, the pincers of a flea,
and all the people, singular and apart. It's not fair,

I know, to let you think I feel no terror.
I can't love what's not here. That's an error.

ON RESUMPTION OF THE
MILITARY DRAFT
(for my student Paul Jolly)

We only want to count you, boys, to find out who
and where you are. We don't need
a draft. We do need to know where we can find you,
just for the files. I wouldn't worry,
it would be a lottery, and you are lucky.
You might as well go down and sign up now.
You must. We only want to count you, boys.
You can't go to Canada anymore,
we've closed the doors. You wouldn't like prison,
you've heard about what goes on in there.
Listen, even if: you don't have to cut your hair.
Don't forget — *there's no war*, no jungles
and gooks. This time it'll be fair,
especially for the niggers and the poor,
who last time, whining, took their simple losses.
We need to know where we can find you.
You need to find: a post office.
Hell, there's no such thing as bayonets
anymore. You never get that close.
Mostly we'd need cooks, and clerks, not many medics,
some maintenance — skilled — and if you're chosen
it's good for the country and for you.
You can do what you want, but it pays
to go along. We don't *need* a war, you know
that won't happen, we had it
with hooch-lightings, leaves and leaf,
green on green, weren't allowed . . .
It's the way we do it and we know how.
We only want to find you, boys, to find out who and,
though it's unlikely we'll need to know, where you are.

WHEN I'M GONE
(for Jean)

Honey, entomb me in honey when I'm gone.
Ancient (Iraqi) practices call for it
and where is it writ that the passed can feel
no pleasure? So poke me down in a golden vat,
there suspend me, eternally, in its sugary ooze.
What better place to sleep a thousand years?
We have to live and we have to die so why not choose
how to spend the lengthier of the two?
Dirt or flames, as alternatives, don't compare.
I suppose the cost could be prohibitive
and think of the wasted work of a billion bees,
but, honey, it *is* a major journey,
and if you seal it tight enough, plug
the top with wax, then it will hold. Think
of the sunlight (the vat, of course, is glass)
washing through, late afternoons, a bowl
of lemons and other fruit, a pretty vase
with flowers standing by . . . This kind of talk
is far from morbid: leaving you I never want to do.
Honey, entomb me in honey when I'm gone.

THE SWIMMING POOL

All around the apt. swimming pool
the boys stare at the girls
and the girls look everywhere but the opposite
or down or up. It is
as it was a thousand years ago: the fat
boy has it hardest, he
takes the sneers,
prefers the winter so he can wear
his heavy pants and sweater.
Today, he's here with the others.
Better they are cruel to him in his presence
than out. Of the five here now (three boys,
two girls) one is fat, three cruel,
and one, a girl, wavers to the side,
all the world tearing at her.
As yet she has no breasts
(her friend does) and were it not
for the forlorn fat boy who she joins
in taunting, she could not bear her terror,
which is the terror
of being him. Does it make her happy
that she has no need, right now, of ingratiation,
of acting fool to salve
her loneliness? She doesn't seem
so happy. She is like
the lower-middle class, that fatal group
handed crumbs so they can drop a few
down lower, to the poor, so they won't kill
the rich. All around
the apt. swimming pool

there is what's everywhere: forsakenness
and fear, a disdain for those beneath us
rather than a rage
against the ones above: the exploiters,
the oblivious and unabashedly cruel.

VIA POSTHUMIA

Narrow street, tiny
hydrants, two-inch
curbs. Where birds
come after a talk
with the feather
merchant, where
the wheat not beaten
into breadflour
goes. In air,
girls, boys, are happy
above skipropes.
A grocer's
peagreen cart: a load
of gray carrots
in the shades.
You'll find rooms to let
near the lampstore
or laundry
where they steam the shrouds.
The neighbors will
be sweet, still,
and if down the lane
you hear firetrucks
or you feel
your heart imploding
you need not fear:
baby street,
gentle
path.

SNAKE LAKE

My friends, I hope you will not swim here:
this lake isn't named for what it lacks.
This is *not* just another vacant scare.
They're in there — knotted, cruel, and thick

with poison, some of them. Others bite
you just for fun — they love that curve
along the white soft side of your foot,
or your lower calf, or to pierce the nerves

with their needles behind your knees.
Just born, the babies bite you all the same.
They don't care how big you are — *please*
do not swim here. There is no shame

in avoiding what will kill you: cool pleasure
of this water. Do not even dip your toes
in because they'll hurt you, or worse,
carry you away on their backs — no,

not in homage, but to bite you as you sink.
Do not, my friends, swim here: I like you
living: this is what I believe, what I think.
Do not swim here — lest the many turn to few.

WIFE HITS MOOSE

Sometime around dusk moose lifts
his heavy, primordial jaw, dripping, from pondwater
and, without psychic struggle,
decides the day, for him, is done: time
to go somewhere else. Meanwhile, wife
drives one of those roads that cut straight north,
a highway dividing the forests

not yet fat enough for the paper companies.
This time of year full dark falls
about eight o'clock — pineforest and blacktop
blend. Moose reaches road, fails
to look both ways, steps
deliberately, ponderously . . . Wife
hits moose, hard,

at slight angle (brakes slammed, car
spinning) and moose rolls over hood, antlers —
as if diamond-tipped — scratch windshield, car
damaged: rib-of-moose imprint
on fender, hoof shatters headlight.
Annoyed moose lands on feet and walks away.
Wife is shaken, unhurt, amazed.

— Does moose believe in a Supreme Intelligence?
Speaker does not know.
— Does wife believe in a Supreme Intelligence?
Speaker assumes as much: spiritual intimacies
being between the spirit and the human.
— Does speaker believe in a Supreme Intelligence?
Yes. Thank You.

PEDESTRIAN

Tottering and elastic, middle name of Groan,
ramfeezled after a hard night
at the corpse-polishing plant, slope-
shouldered, a half loaf
of bread, even his hair tired, famished,
fingering the diminished beans
in his pocket — you meet him.
On a thousand street corners you meet him,
emerging from the subway, emerging
from your own chest — this sight's shrill,
metallic vapors pass into you.
His fear is of being broken,
of becoming *too* dexterous in stripping
the last few shoelaces of meat
from a chicken's carcass, of being moved by nothing
short of the Fall of Rome, of being stooped
in the cranium over some loss he's forgotten
the anniversary of . . . You meet him,
know his defeat, though proper
and inevitable, is not yours, although yours also
is proper and inevitable: so many defeats
queer and insignificant (as illustration:
the first time you lay awake all night
waiting for dawn — and were disappointed), so many
no-hope exhaustions hidden,
their gaze dully glazed inward — And yet we all
fix our binoculars on the horizon's hazy fear-heaps
and cruise toward them, fat sails
forward . . . You meet him on the corners,

in bus stations, on the blind avenues
leading neither in
nor out of hell, you meet him
and with him you walk.

IV

TRIPTYCH, MIDDLE PANEL BURNING

1

It happened that my uncle liked to take my hand in his
and with the other seize
the electric cow fence: a little rural
humor, don't get me wrong

no way child abuse. He
took the voltage first
and besides it only slaps and never burns,
or even seems to bother

the cows. It's merely a small snake
flying up your arm (it feels most
peculiar at the first wrist), across
your shoulders (there's a slight

buzzing, though, still in your top
vertebra), and down
the other until it — the shock — explodes
at the end of each of your five free

fingertips. Thank you, Uncle.
You made sure I'd never murder — not
after they fried the guys who deserved it
in the movies. Society, and I, thank you.

You also kept me from the mental hospitals
when that was all in fashion — for fear
of the electrodes to my temples. And thus,
you saved me and my insurance carriers

some money so we could buy more goods,
which is good for all of us. Thanks. I count
it as a normal childhood, so prosaic
the traumas — say, a live, for several hours,

Japanese beetle wedged beneath a cast
on a broken arm — that only once did I fully believe
in God: when He clearly punished me
for a stupid and embarrassing act

of cruelty. I liked it fine alone
amidst the asunder of a purely American loneliness:
a decline of conscience simultaneously
with the instinctual conscience of a child's

trying to form. It was 1955
and America was as arrogant as it ever gets;
we'd polished off a few wars, a lot
of our fathers were gone for good

and we were ready for what matters: lucra-
tive employ, bomb shelters, a few scoots
in the bank, babies, a fat Sunday
dinner. Art didn't matter much, so what,

nor generosity. We, as a nation, earned
our ignorance and the right to pass it on.
— These memories are so banal and so sweet
they almost *attack* me: How I survived

a pitchfork tossed at my chest, how I survived
(with more difficulty) algebra's x's and y's,
how the hayfields hid me, how the perfume-bottle-cleaved
smell of a fresh-plowed field or a field

after first thin snowfall spread
with hot manure made me feel *perfectly*
alive. Even what died
did not bother me — I understood

that simple reality. When I came across
the severed head (a neat powder-burned
pencil-sized hole between its wide eyes) and legs,
and entrails, and tail of a cow I'd fed

through a spring, summer, and winter,
I understood. I knew where stew meat
and flank steak came from, and though
I liked that Angus I was pleased

to see that, in fact, they *do* have three stomachs.
Her face, I admit, looked surprised — not
bloody and so neatly severed — and I tested
its heaviness to see if I could carry it,

under my arm, to school. I even understood
and appreciated the meatflies' swarm
and ecstasy. I poked the bellies
with a stick — they were blue — and figured

it was time to smoke the cigar I'd filched
somewhere. As I said, it was a normal
childhood, but still I was astounded
by ignorance — my own — and by what I guessed

was missing. What America stressed was: engineers
we need; money happy, and otherwise it don't matter
so long as you don't cause trouble. Once
I saw the near-idiot neighbor boy rape

a chicken, killing it, and judging
by the noise, causing it great pain as well.
He never felt so smart and I could tell
he liked being in charge, knowing what, for once,

he was doing. Later, he told his father
it was the fox come again and could he kill it
too? His father sadly and savagely beat him
with a rake. I thought I could teach

this boy to read — until he set the books on fire.
It was never that I ever thought: what
am *I* doing here, me, one of the sensitives;
it was more: this is exactly where I *do*

belong, this is it as it truly exists.
And when I would stare into the coals
after a family barbeque the dull orange glow
seemed to me as beautiful as color

ever gets. The midsummer evening chill
would descend on my arms and not once
did I ever fear death, or life. Hay smell
was everywhere, Lord Jesus, we had the third-best

water in these United States, two wars over,
my sweet father still intact,
my mother strong and never
oppressed, and yet I knew something was wrong

as well as I knew something was right.

2

Is true that you get born dumb and bald as a ball-
peen hammer and as bald
and dumb you expire. So it's. In between,
you choose to live in a manner you can live with,
you build what you can build, and you learn,
as Mr. Stevens says, you learn to reject
the trash. And down it goes here: the rage
and ugly of that trash, the noisome,
the suppuration and putrid: *that which will not
do*. Like a bad black piece of cheese you want to give back

all the lies and crooked imaginings — as green,
loose, and valuable as duck drops, all the sad
homilies, like noses with a thousand pustules, pustules
on top of pustules (like folding campcups),
the knitting needles plunged into your ear
to quiet the mind's terrible machine,
the singular obsessions endlessly revised: the design
of a mummy case, all that business
about the Sandman, how he puts you to sleep
(Who wouldn't under dunes of it?)
and then coins like sandbags piled up
against false flood: you have to pass it back
to your fathers, your slaves, to your baby bonnets
deranged — so that the bad half
of an idiot savant you won't be: you have to pass it *back*,
not on: all the fat and artless, all
creation unable to escape a niggardly self,

all the art of brilliant solipsism, all scrofulous
associations with *fine* wine or haute couture
and the attendant doilylike sophistications,
the exclusives beating the poor to death
with crystal fingerbowls, spearing
them with diamond stickpins: the humiliation
of poverty: you must
give it back — no man or woman should feel
it — like a hypodermic needle broken off
at skin level, and then another and another
until there's a beard of them, a *physical*
humiliation: no one should be forced
to bake bread with scraps and burnt matches:
nothing like *odium dei* do I call for,
only some way to say to each other: a higher
power controls me and I invented it to be gentler
than yours — my power gentler than yours!: I say
what I reject most is adamant self-love
and self-justification — in all their costumes,
those cruel constructions of suet: I spit
on the lapel of a pompous man because he robs
another of self and himself of dignity, I spit
on the lugubrious surveyors of personal internal
disaster areas calling for federal help,
the self-hagiographers, those who crush
the blooming milt's possibilities in the same way
every (every!) kindergarten — vessel for shame — child
in America is told and told again to imagine
that imagination is something to be dispensed
with: I'm rattling with rage over what I simply

want to reject: not only the wearing
of your victim's toes and ears around your neck
but also the position you have to put him in
to take them, not only dread but also its rancid
chopping block with blood pounded
into its grain, not only the cruelty
of inarticulated love, or sex, but also selfishness
of tongues, not only colossal indifference
but also its cause, not only shark attacks but also
their really rubber teeth: I won't
accept it anymore, I reject
it: the cruelty of aggression and the cruelty
of withdrawal, love with hard bark
on it, a grueling insistence of form,
loverboy, greasy mongrels of the groin — let me
be not distant, nor man nor woman from me,
let me not need to write palinode after palinode,
let me take rage and divide it
again and again until is left one grain upon my palm
to blow away — cruelty and stupidity — and soon
I shall crawl out of a great pit, soon
I will crawl its slimy walls
out, fierce toeholds holding, little helpful
hooks my fingernails — it's got to be rejected:
blueprints too blue, architects building barracks
for peasants to live in
while they build mansions for generals, the peasants'
gruel and its lumps accepted as course,
the beautiful verses filled
with vermin, the sad devotion of flagellants,

the stupefacients fed us daily,
the quotidian humiliations and the rare
humiliations, all that which causes
the terrors, the bloody taciturnity, all
the blink-blown, irrevocable severings . . .

If there are, each day, terrors
we have to live with
let them be: that we fail to *make*
something (*anything*, in whatever
realm: a new lilypad,
a way to line one extra belly
with nutrients, a tool
to scan and receive the vision of God);
and, of course, of course: that we not
be able to love.

3

It's clear: a future, there should be
a future. Once he was (he was!) drawn to,
devotedly, the recondites of death,
another side. He thought it absorbing
and only didn't like that he could go there one-way

only. It was a thrill to hit 100 m.p.h., slam
his eyes, and count off seconds: 3, 4, 5
while standing harder on the pedal — a kind
of sad, athletic exercise. No longer
does he indulge in that. In fact, he'd like back

those doltish days wasted
in pursuit of erasure. But there's no fruit
in that longing: blanks gone
are gone, the seeds in the doom rattle
settle — silent, level. What shivers

of loathing that remain are bell-beacons clanging
happily above a reef's razors. It's enough
that he's waived the hard slide
down a frozen chute. There's no need to hurry
it — oblivion — since for us it comes

on its own time: passive, patient, neverminding
our white and bloody knees.
He won't listen to poems anymore

about the other shore and its sweetnesses
(their original points that he missed?)

nor does he care about the obvious or bland
alternatives: Oh, a little house, power,
a piece of land. He wants to own nothing
but his heartbone banging, born of anything.
He doesn't want a little wife, he wants a *big*

wife and he wants their babies
dancing with Daddy alert as an eland,
dancing with Daddy divested of fear,
dancing with Daddy lucidly, lucidly, clear.
Of the past he can't change one hair,

the future he can't invent and will be wary
even in dreaming it.
It's like this: a speaker
has the moment in which he speaks — and that
is a raging, bloom-sodden abundance: a dilated sky

crammed with air (but its outer-
zoned, infinity-harking edges eaten
by Zyklon B, rads, megatons . . .) wholly
breathable, the heart and lungs perpetual
machines ready to run, eyelids lifting

like birds off cool water . . . One can choose
to live on this orb or die

on it: between the two
he's no longer shredded. — In a papery pinnace,
a twine-bound flyboat, he circled

a teetering globe: a long winter chewing
his shoes at Port Famine, several months tapping
his cane around *Isla Desolación*, a hundred
heated nights huddling through dead
calms. The best burning ground he leased,

piled the kindling chin-high (powdered with resin,
soaked in pitch), tortured and confessed,
and invited a crowd to his own at-the-stake;
his own buboes, blisters he abetted,
and blains. Quenchless, he stood

berating no one (a flat pan of warm-
as-bathwater bay before him), berating what he could see
of the moor, the night.
Pure peroration, his head shaved
and with a bull's eye painted

on his bitten skull. If there was an answer
he could not hear it.
Supercilious, blind and writhing
like a maggot in a hogshead of filet mignon,
he said: Bring it down, loose your toothiest landslide,

Lord, I want it, I'll take all the aches
you have, give it to me open-bore

and wide-pattern — so I can go . . . But
for whatever reasons his pieces
were not snatched up by Whosoever's talons

and dropped on rocks washed pale
by bird dust. For whatever reason was offered,
and he took: manumission, a sliver
at first, then a wider crack, then wider
into which he wedged a bony hip, and then more

open, like an *O*, a circle, not
a zero, and there was one whiff
of sweet air. It was not a paradise
he got a glimpse of, it was of *this*
world, an incessant reality, a multi-edged

wholeness. And it will do. It will do.
It was not for lack of trying he did not die.
Wavering, the patient suddenly
took a turn toward better, the crinkling
oxygen tent filled with blue light

(in a bearded God he doesn't believe,
nor in the crows who serve him) — there was just
a little light: electrical, metaphysical,
mizzling on a thousand pinpoints;
no symbol like an *X* burned his forehead,

there was a coin of light; no voice inside
or further inside, not one choirboy did appear;

it was only a light made up of particles of light,
it was just a black table soaked
in light and then the black broke down,

split apart, dispersed with a purpose — like drops
of blood borne off a battlefield
on the backs of ants, and following: rain, rain.

Waynesburg College Library
Waynesburg, Pa.   15370